The Ghost House

Contents

FULL FLIGHT >> runway >>>

Titles in the Runway series

Badger Publishing Limited
15 Wedgwood Gate, Pin Green Industrial Estate,
Stevenage, Hertfordshire SG1 4SU
Telephone: 01438 356907, Fax: 01438 747015
www.badger-publishing.co.uk
enquiries@badger-publishing.co.uk

The Ghost House ISBN 978 1 84691 368 6

Text © Keith West and Alison Hawes 2008
Complete work © Badger Publishing Limited 2008

Publisher: David Jamieson
Commissioning Editor: Carrie Lewis
Design: Fiona Grant
Illustration: Oliver Lake, Aleksandar Sotirovski, Robin Lawrie

Printed and bound in China through Colorcraft Ltd., Hong Kong

>>The Ghost House

Written by Keith West
Illustrated by Oliver Lake

The gang were after Kermal.
He had to hide.

He ran into an old house.
People said the house was haunted.

He ran up the old stairs.
The gang were still after him.

Kermal ran into a room.
There was an old man.
The old man pointed under the bed.

"Thank you," said Kermal.
He hid under the bed.

The gang ran into the room.
They saw the old man.

The old man had no eyes.
The gang ran out of the house.

Kermal came out from under the bed.
There was no old man.
There was just a pile of old clothes.

The Lie

Written by Alison Hawes
Illustrated by Aleksander Sotirovski

The soldiers came to the village.
They looked in the houses.

The soldiers put the men and women into trucks.

The soldiers looked in the bedrooms.
They looked in the bathrooms.

They looked in the kitchens.
They looked in the attics.

One soldier looked in a big cellar.
He saw all the children.

The soldier remembered when he was a child.

He remembered when he hid from the soldiers.

The soldier closed the cellar door.

This house is empty

Let's go!

Ella's Room

Written by Alison Hawes
Illustrated by Robin Lawrie

Ella's room was a mess!

Her clothes were on the floor.
Her CDs were on the floor.

Ella's mum yelled,
"Tidy up your room, Ella!"

But Ella's room was still a mess.

Ella's mum stopped Ella's pocket money.
But Ella's room was still a mess!

Then one day Ella's room was tidy.
"Your room is tidy!" said Ella's mum.

Ella's sister said, "I know why Ella's room is tidy."

"Why?" said mum.

"Ella wants a TV in her room," said Ella's sister.

"Dad said okay.
But only if her room was NOT a mess!"

>>> Vocabulary

The Ghost House

gang
hide
house
haunted
stairs
room
pointed
bed
pile
clothes

The Lie

soldiers
village
children
trucks
lying
bedrooms
bathrooms
kitchens
attics
cellar

remembered
door
empty

Ella's Room

mess
floor
CDs
yelled
tidy
pocket money
TV

>>> Story questions

The Ghost House

Who was after Kermal?
Who was already in the room that Kermal ran into?
Who do you think the old man was?

The Lie

What were the soldiers looking for?
Where were the children hiding?
Why did the soldier tell a lie?

Ella's Room

What did Ella's mum want Ella to do?
How did Ella's mum try to make her tidy her room?
Why did Ella tidy her room in the end?